HEINEMANN
STATE STUDIES

Uniquely
Georgia

Larry Bograd

Heinemann Library
Chicago, Illinois

© 2004 Heinemann Library
a division of Reed Elsevier Inc.
Chicago, Illinois

Customer Service 888-454-2279

Visit our website at www.heinemannlibrary.com

Designed by Heinemann Library
Printed in China by WKT Company Limited.

07 06 05 04
10 9 8 7 6 5 4 3 2 1

**Library of Congress
Cataloging-in-Publication Data**

Bograd, Larry.
  Uniquely Georgia / Larry Bograd.
    p. cm. — (Heinemann state studies)
Summary: Discusses the people, land and climate,
history, culture, and economy of Georgia, as well as
other aspects of the state that make it unique.
Includes bibliographical references and index.
  ISBN 1-4034-4489-7 (HC library binding) —
ISBN 1-4034-4504-4 (PB)
  1. Georgia—Juvenile literature. [1. Georgia.]
I. Title. II. Series.
  F286.3.B64 2003
  975.8—dc22

                                        2003014332

Acknowledgments
Development and photo research by
BOOK BUILDERS LLC

The author and publishers are grateful to the
following for permission to reproduce copyright
material:

Cover photographs by (top, L-R): Georgia
Department of Industry, Trade, and Tourism;
Panoramic Images www.panoramicimages.com;
Flip Schulke/CORBIS; Owaki-Kulla/CORBIS; (main)
Carl Purcell/Photo Researchers Inc.

Title page (L, M): Georgia Department of Industry,
Trade, and Tourism; (R) Andre Jenny/Alamy
Images; Contents page: Georgia Department of
Industry, Trade, and Tourism; pp. 4, 25 Andre
Jenny/Alamy Images; 5 Carl Purcell/Photo
Researchers Inc.; pp. 6, 7, 9, 13T, 13M, 14B, 17,
22B, 26, 27, 29, 30, 31, 35, 38, 40, 41, 43
Georgia Department of Industry, Trade, and
Tourism; pp. 8, 42, 45 maps by IMA for Book
Builders LLC; p. 10 Courtesy Spelman College;
p. 11T Panoramic Images www.panoramicimages
.com; p. 13B Robert Harding World Imagery/
Alamy Images; p. 14T Dr. Suresh Vasant/Alamy
Images; p. 15T Ron and Valerie Taylor/Alamy
Images; p. 15M Andrew Prokos Photography/
Alamy Images; p. 15B USFWS/Washington D.C.
Library; p. 16T Carmela Leszczynski/
AnimalsAnimals; pp. 19, 20 22T, 23T, 24 Culver
Pictures; p. 23B Flip Schulke/CORBIS; p. 32
B. Minton/Heinemann Library; p. 34 R.
Capozzelli/Heinemann Library; p. 36 Jimmy Cribb;
p. 37 Courtesy UGA Sports Communications; p. 39
Owaki-Kulla/CORBIS; p. 44 Courtesy Tubman
African American Museum.

Special thanks to Steve Potts of Hibbing
Community College for his expert comments in
the preparation of this book.

Every effort has been made to contact copyright
holders of any material reproduced in this book.
Any omissions will be rectified in subsequent
printings if notice is given to the publisher.

Cover Pictures

Top (left to right) State capitol building in
Atlanta, Martin Luther King Jr., Georgia state
flag, farmer with Vadalia sweet onions **Main**
Historic home in Savannah

Some words are shown in bold, **like this**.
You can find out what they mean by looking
in the glossary.

Contents

Uniquely Georgia

Unique means one of a kind. And that describes Georgia, the largest state east of the Mississippi River. Named for King George II of England, who granted land to Georgia's original colonists, Georgia has a lot packed within its borders. Atlanta, which hosted the 1996 Olympic games, is Georgia's state capital and largest city. Savannah, founded in 1733, is one of the oldest cities in the South. Jimmy Carter, the first president elected from the South since the **Civil War** (1861–1865), is from Georgia.

MAJOR CITIES

Founded in 1837 Atlanta is located in the north-central part of the state. In 1864 during the Civil War, the Battle of Atlanta took place, which resulted in most of the city burning to the ground. Today, Atlanta is home to nearly 400,000 people and to Hartsfield-Jackson Atlanta International Airport, the busiest airport in the world in terms of passengers. The city is also the headquarters of the Cable News Network (CNN), the cable TV news

Atlanta is Georgia's largest city and the state capital. Many of the buildings that make up the Atlanta skyline were designed by graduates from Georgia Tech.

Savannah's urban historic district is the largest in the nation.

channel, and to one of the most famous drinks in the world, Coca-Cola.

Savannah, on Georgia's Atlantic coast, is called the "Hostess City of the South" because its residents go out of their way to make visitors feel welcome. More than 130,000 people live there. The city's origin dates to 1733 when the British general James Oglethorpe landed on a **bluff** above the Savannah River. Oglethorpe designed the city to be a series of square-shaped parks and neighborhoods. Today, the city is filled with enormous oak trees and sweet-smelling plants, such as jasmine and azalea. During the early 1800s, Savannah was a port where cotton was shipped from the United States to England and other countries. As a result, the most successful cotton merchants became rich and built mansions, many of which can be seen today.

The city of Columbus sits on the Chattahoochee River, at the western border of Georgia, 95 miles southwest of Atlanta. It was founded in 1828 as a shipping center for cotton that was making its way by boat to New Orleans. Local merchants then decided to build mills where cotton was turned into cloth and thread because there was more money to be made with finished goods than with raw cotton. Today, it is home to 275,000 people, making it Georgia's second-largest city. Because of its many mills, Columbus is the denim-producing capital of the world. Denim is the cloth used to make jeans. Columbus is also home to Fort Benning, the largest **infantry** school in the world. The U.S. Army's infantry are headquartered at Fort Benning.

Georgia's Geography and Climate

Georgia is divided into five major land regions. From northwest to southeast, they are the Valley and Ridge, the Blue Ridge, the Piedmont, the Fall Line Hills, and the Coastal Plains.

LAND

The Valley and Ridge is made of **ancient** rocks that are more than 100 million years old. The rocks were shaped into the many valleys and ridges that give the region its name. This region makes up the northwest corner of Georgia and spreads into Alabama and Tennessee. Coal is mined in this region.

Lookout Mountain

Lookout Mountain is located in northwestern Georgia. This enormous mountain is so large that its base is located in three different states: Georgia, Tennessee, and Alabama. It is the only mountain in the country that covers parts of three states. Here, archeologists have found bones of ancient Native Americans that date back to about 200 B.C.E. Today, visitors can ride a mile up the mountain on the world's steepest inclined train, where they can overlook the Tennessee River Valley.

The Blue Ridge region is part of the Appalachians. At about 480 million years old, they are the oldest mountains in the world. They stretch from Maine to Alabama. In the 1820s gold was discovered near the town of Dahlonega. There was so much gold that the U.S. government operated a **mint** there from 1830 to 1861 that made gold coins. Georgia's highest point is also part of this region. Brasstown Bald is a mountain that reaches 4,784 feet above sea level. It is called "bald" because its treeless rounded top looks like the top of a bald head.

The Piedmont region consists mostly of rolling hills, pine forests, and raised flat areas called plateaus. Atlanta is located on the Central Piedmont Plateau. The Piedmont makes up nearly one-third of the state. Its soil is usually the red color of clay. Quarry workers remove large slabs of granite from the eastern Piedmont. The granite is used for tombstones and monuments. A famous landmark in this region, the **Confederate** Memorial Carving, is a statue carved into the granite of Stone Mountain, which is north of Atlanta. It depicts Jefferson Davis, Robert E. Lee, and Thomas "Stonewall" Jackson, leaders of the Southern states during the **Civil War**.

The Fall Line Hills separate the Piedmont and the Coastal Plains and cover about one-fourth of the state. Its name comes from the many waterfalls and river **rapids** found there. The cities of Columbus and Macon, which is in central Georgia, developed along the Chattahoochee and Ocmulgee Rivers in this region.

Storms from the Gulf of Mexico travel north over the Coastal Plains and into the rest of the state.

The Coastal Plains, or flatlands, stretch across southern Georgia. Part of this region reaches south toward the Gulf of Mexico. The other part moves east toward the Atlantic Ocean. One of Georgia's most unique attractions, the

Okefenokee Swamp, is located in the Coastal Plains. It is one of the largest freshwater **wetlands** in the world. Preserved as a national wildlife refuge, the swamp is home to numerous birds, panthers, crocodiles, and countless cypress and live oak trees.

CLIMATE

Climate is the pattern of a region's temperature, wind, and amount of rainfall. Climate is observed over many years. The southern states are warmer than the northern states because they are closer to the equator, or the earth's middle.

Winter is short and mild, and temperatures rarely dip below 32°F. The Valley and Ridge and the Blue Ridge Mountains receive what little snow falls on the state. It rains year-round. Because winter is short, spring is in full bloom by March. Summer lasts through September, and temperatures are in the 80s and 90s.

On average, the state receives 40 to 50 inches of rain each year.

Average Annual Precipitation Georgia

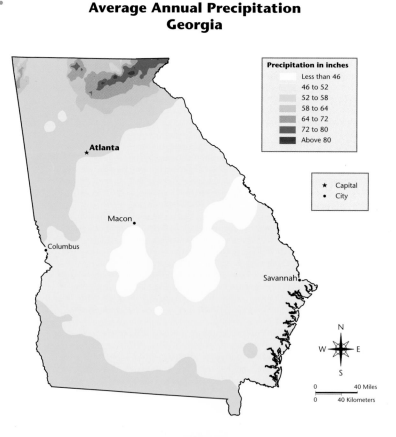

Precipitation in inches

	Less than 46
	46 to 52
	52 to 58
	58 to 64
	64 to 72
	72 to 80
	Above 80

★ Capital
• City

Atlanta
Macon
Columbus
Savannah

N
W — E
S

0   40 Miles
0   40 Kilometers

Famous Firsts

FIRSTS OF THE 1700S

In 1736, just three years after Georgia was established as a colony, the first **Protestant** Sunday school was founded in Savannah. In the same year the first golf course in North America opened near Savannah.

In 1785 Georgia became the first state of the original thirteen colonies to form a state-supported university. The University of Georgia was established by an act of the state's governing body called the General Assembly, signaling Georgia's commitment to higher education.

FIRSTS OF THE 1800S

In 1803 Sarah Porter Hillhouse became the first woman in the United States to edit, publish, and own a newspaper. She ran the *Washington Gazette* newspaper for more than ten years.

The first buildings at the University of Georgia were constructed in 1801 on the banks of the Oconee River.

Mined gold is usually mixed with other minerals. Miners must remove these minerals before the gold may be used. Therefore, gold that is mostly pure is more valuable than less pure gold. The purest gold in the world was found in Dahlonega in 1828. A year later, after word spread of the discovery, thousands of people rushed to the area hoping to find gold. This became the first gold rush in the United States.

Spelman College is a private, liberal arts college for African American women. In 1992 it was named the top regional liberal arts college in the South by U.S. News & World Report.

In 1866 Georgia became the first state to give women full property rights, meaning that a woman could own a home, farm, or business on her own, with or without a husband. Previously, women were restricted to the home, serving as wife and mother. In 1881 Spelman College in Atlanta became the first college and nursing school established for African American women.

FIRSTS OF THE 1900s

In 1912 the first Girl Scouts of America meeting took place in the Savannah home of Juliette Gordon Low. At that time the group had only eighteen members and called itself the Girl Guides. Today, the Girl Scouts is the world's largest organization for girls. There are more than ten million Girl Scouts and Girl Guides in 144 countries.

In 1931 passenger planes were a rare and expensive form of transportation. Atlanta's airport became the first to have a passenger terminal, where people could wait to board planes. In 1956, as more people took to the air, the airport became the first place to land a passenger jet, a French Caravelle. Previously, jet planes had been reserved for military use.

In 1943 Georgia became the first state to give eighteen year olds the right to vote in state elections. Previously, citizens had to be 21 years old to vote. This landmark decision led other states to do the same.

Georgia's State Symbols

GEORGIA STATE FLAG

In 2003 Georgia adopted a new state flag, replacing one adopted in 2001. The 2001 flag had replaced one used since 1956 that represented the state's **Confederate** past and legacy of **slavery**.

However, the 2001 flag was unpopular. People thought it was poorly designed because it included a row of five smaller flags. The new flag highlights the state seal surrounded by thirteen stars, representing Georgia's role as one of the country's original states.

The current state flag will be approved by voters in the 2004 presidential election.

GEORGIA STATE SEAL

The state seal was designed in 1798. On its front side are three pillars supporting an arch. Each pillar represents one of the three branches of government—the legislative, judicial, and executive.

STATE MOTTO: "WISDOM, JUSTICE, AND MODERATION"

Georgia's state motto is "Wisdom, Justice, and Moderation." Wisdom means knowledge and good judgment gained over time.

By law, the Georgia secretary of state is the official keeper of the state seal, which is used on official papers and orders.

Justice means living by a set of laws based on fair treatment. Moderation means neither too much nor too little but rather a balanced amount of effort.

STATE NICKNAME: THE PEACH STATE

Georgia does not have an official nickname. Among the nicknames often used to describe it are "The Peach State," "The Goober State," and "The Empire State of the South." The first two nicknames refer to two of Georgia's leading products, peaches and goobers—another name for peanuts. The third nickname refers to Georgia's central role to its region's business, because Atlanta is a banking and transportation hub.

STATE SONG: "GEORGIA ON MY MIND"

The state song, "Georgia on My Mind," was written in 1930 by Stuart Gorrell and Hoagy Carmichael. Many singers have recorded the song, but it became world famous when sung by music legend Ray Charles in the 1950s. In 1979 the state **legislature** selected it as the state song. By law, if someone uses the song for state business, it must be the version sung by Ray Charles.

"Georgia on My Mind"

Melodies bring memories
That linger in my heart
Make me think of Georgia
Why did we ever part?
Some sweet day when blossoms fall
And all the world's a song
I'll go back to Georgia
'Cause that's where I belong.

Georgia, Georgia, the whole day through
Just an old sweet song keeps Georgia on
   my mind.
Georgia, Georgia, a song of you
Comes as sweet and clear as moonlight
   through the pines.
Other arms reach out to me
Other eyes smile tenderly
Still in peaceful dreams I see
The road leads back to you.

Georgia, Georgia, no peace I find
Just an old sweet song keeps Georgia on
   my mind.

STATE FLOWER: CHEROKEE ROSE

In 1916 the Cherokee rose was named the state flower. Its name comes from the Cherokee people who planted the rose throughout the state. The rose flower is white and has a large golden center. The Cherokee believe the white color represents the tears shed by their people who suffered at the hands of settlers. The gold represents the gold taken from Cherokee lands in the first half of the 1800s.

The Cherokee rose blooms in the early spring. It will bloom a second time, in the fall, if the weather is warm enough.

STATE TREE: LIVE OAK

In 1937 the live oak was adopted as the official state tree. Mostly it grows along the sandy soils of the Coastal Plains. This tree grows 60 to 80 feet in height and can be easily **transplanted**. It gets its name because its leaves stay green year-round.

STATE BIRD: BROWN THRASHER

In 1935 the brown thrasher was selected by the governor as the Georgia state bird. It was not until 1970, however, that the legislature voted it the official state bird. Almost a foot in length, the brown thrasher has a long curved bill and a long tail. Its wings have two white bars. Its body is brown, and its white breast is streaked with brown.

People use the live oak mostly for decoration. Birds and animals eat the tree's acorns.

The brown thrasher can be found in the eastern United States. The bird migrates north to Canada in the summer and spends the winter in Georgia and other southern states.

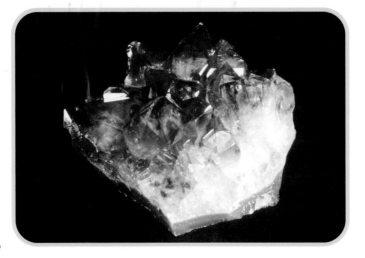

Two types of quartz are common in Georgia. Amethyst, a purple quartz, is used in jewelry. Clear quartz, once it is cut and polished, looks like a diamond. It also is used in jewelry.

STATE GEMSTONE: QUARTZ

In 1976 quartz became the official state gem. It is found throughout Georgia in such colors as white, pink, and brown.

STATE MINERAL: STAUROLITE

In 1976 staurolite was named the official state mineral. Popular names for this mineral include "fairy crosses" and "fairy stones." Most often found in northern Georgia, staurolite is collected and used for good luck charms.

The right whale is the only whale that is native to Georgia's waters.

STATE MAMMAL: RIGHT WHALE

The right whale was named by hunters because it was the "right" whale to hunt for oil used in lamps. In the early 1980s scientists discovered that the water off Georgia's Atlantic coast was a place where many right whales were born. This type of whale is an **endangered** species. In 1985 the right whale became the state marine mammal. The right whale grows up to 50 feet long

STATE INSECT: HONEYBEE

The honeybee was selected as the official state insect in 1975. It is a member of one of the largest insect families, which has 20,000 other species. Honeybees are highly social. A single colony or hive usually contains one queen that lays the eggs, 50,000 **worker bees**, and a hundred or so **drones**. Georgia farmers and beekeepers make money by selling honey and wax made by honeybees.

STATE FOSSIL: SHARK TOOTH

In 1976 the shark tooth became the official state fossil. It is a common fossil in the Georgia Coastal Plain. People walking on the beach often find it. Sharks have lived in and near Georgia for around 275 million years.

Fossilized shark teeth are found in a range of colors. The common colors are black, gray, white, brown, and blue.

STATE BUTTERFLY: TIGER SWALLOWTAIL

The tiger swallowtail became the state butterfly in 1988. It is one of the most common butterflies in the eastern United States. John White, an English explorer, did the first drawing of a North American swallowtail in 1587.

STATE FISH: LARGEMOUTH BASS

In 1970 the largemouth bass was named Georgia's state fish. According to the bill that made the largemouth bass the state fish, Georgia is world famous as a "fisherman's paradise" that produced the world's largest largemouth bass.

Its black and yellow color explains why this butterfly is named "tiger." The name "swallowtail" comes from the long pointed tail that resembles the tail belonging to a bird called a swallow.

The largemouth bass eats other fish and crayfish, a small shrimp-like creature.

The gopher tortoise is so named because it has shovel-like front arms and it burrows like a gopher into sandy soil to make its home.

George W. Perry, a nineteen-year-old farmer, caught the 22-pound fish in 1932, a record that stood for more than 50 years.

STATE REPTILE: GOPHER TORTOISE

The gopher tortoise is the largest land turtle in the South and the oldest living species native to Georgia. It averages between six and nine inches in length, and some tortoises measure more than a foot. It was once found throughout the Coastal Plains of southern Georgia. Because humans took over much of the land, the number of gopher tortoises has dwindled. To help restore its numbers, the federal and state government listed the gopher tortoise as a **threatened species**.

The Georgia state quarter was issued in 1999. It was the fourth state quarter, matching Georgia's place as the fourth state to become part of the United States.

STATE VEGETABLE: VIDALIA SWEET ONION

In the spring of 1931 onion grower Mose Coleman tasted one of his crop, expecting it to be hot like other onions. Instead, it had a sweet taste. He grew more sweet onions and started selling them. Neighboring farmers joined in, taking their harvest to the town of Vidalia in south-central Georgia. Soon people from near and far traveled to Vidalia just to buy these unusual onions. Today, the name Vidalia Sweet is reserved only for onions grown in twenty Georgia counties. It became the state vegetable in 1990.

GEORGIA STATE QUARTER

The backside of the Georgia quarter uses several state symbols. The state fruit, the peach, is in the center, in front of an outline of the state of Georgia. Live oak branches border the peach. The state motto, "Wisdom, Justice, Moderation," is shown on a banner draped across the top.

Georgia's History & People

Human history in present-day Georgia dates back about 12,000 years. As one of the original thirteen colonies, its state history dates from the earliest days of the country.

EARLY PEOPLE

It is likely that Georgia's first people were hunters following herds of large animals through the region. About 3,000 years ago, Native Americans began to build villages and large mounds out of dirt. They used these mounds for religious purposes and burials. Several of these ancient mounds remain in Georgia. The largest mound is found near Cartersville in the northern part of the state. It stands more than 60 feet tall, has a flat top, and covers three acres. Pieces of pottery, arrowheads, and bones can still be found at the mounds.

NATIVE AMERICANS

By 1500 there were two main Native American tribes in what is now Georgia: the Creek and the Cherokee. The Creek lived in the lower Piedmont region and Coastal Plains. They were named the Creek because Spanish ex-

The central, or temple, mound was a place where Native Americans held religious ceremonies.

The Talking Leaves—the First Native American Alphabet

Sequoyah, a Cherokee born in 1776, believed that a key to the Cherokee nation's survival was its ability to read and write its native language. Sequoyah was a silversmith. One of his customers suggested that he sign his handmade jewelry. Sequoyah went to an English settler, who showed him how his name would look in English. This inspired him to create a written alphabet, because, like most Native American languages, the Cherokee language lacked one. Sequoyah took twelve years to create one. The alphabet used a different written symbol, or letter, for each sound in the Cherokee language. Sequoyah called these 85 letters "talking leaves" to make fun of white settlers. He believed that settlers' words were like dried leaves that meant nothing and easily blew away. Using Sequoyah's alphabet, the Cherokee could read and write their language, and they produced the first Native American newspaper *The Cherokee Phoenix* in 1828.

plorers found them living alongside rivers and streams. The Cherokee lived in the north and were the largest tribe in the area. At first, both tribes tried to live with the increasing number of European settlers. But by the early 1800s, the U.S. Army had forced the Creek and the Cherokee out of the region.

SPANISH EXPLORERS AND FORTS

In 1540 a Spanish explorer named Hernando de Soto and an army of 600 men came up from present-day Florida into Georgia. They explored the area for gold and other resources. They never found gold, but they spread new diseases among the native people, whose bodies were unable to defend them against illness. Thousands died as a result.

ENGLISH EXPLORATION AND SETTLEMENT

By the early 1700s English settlers had established a colony in present-day South Carolina. A group of them moved south to widen the colony down the coast and build Fort

King George at the Savannah River, near present-day Savannah. Feeling isolated from their countrymen, this small group abandoned the fort in 1727. A larger group of English settlers, led by James Oglethorpe, arrived near Savannah in 1733 and stayed. Oglethorpe, a wealthy English politician, provided each colonist with a year of supplies, such as farming equipment and food, and 50 acres of land.

*James Oglethorpe was able to add more land to his **charter** by making peace with the Creek.*

AMERICAN REVOLUTION AND STATEHOOD

Although most English settlers in Georgia remained loyal colonists to King George II, from 1750 to 1776, many U.S. colonists began to dislike laws and taxes imposed on them by the king. By 1776 the majority of the colonists wanted to create their own country, and they declared their independence from England. The king sent troops to North America to put down the rebellion.

The Revolutionary War, or the War of American Independence, began in 1775. English troops invaded Georgia and captured Savannah in December 1778. By capturing the colony's main city and port, the English controlled all of Georgia, because they cut off supplies shipped along the Atlantic coast. In 1781 the Revolutionary War ended with the U.S. victory at the Battle of Yorktown, Virginia. The defeated English army returned to England. On January 2, 1788, Georgia became the fourth of the original thirteen states that made up the United States.

KING COTTON AND SLAVERY

English colonists had brought cotton, along with rice and tobacco, to Georgia. The demand for cotton increased. By

Eli Whitney finished making his first cotton gin after only ten days of work.

1850 cotton made up two-thirds of American **exports**. It became Georgia's most important moneymaker.

Landowners brought African **slaves** to Georgia to work in the fields. Most slaves lived on large plantations, or estates, located on the Coastal Plains.

The cotton business underwent an enormous change in 1793. That year Eli Whitney invented the cotton gin on a plantation on the Savannah River. This small hand-cranked machine separated the cotton balls from their sharp pods and numerous seeds. It saved time and effort. However, it also increased the demand for slaves to work the fields. Now more cotton could be planted because the gin made it easier to take it from the field to the market.

THE TRAIL OF TEARS

In the first half of the 1800s, Native Americans shared the land that also was claimed by settlers. The situation reached a crisis after gold was discovered in northern Georgia in 1828. Prospectors, or gold seekers, poured into Georgia. The Cherokee asked the U.S. Congress for protection from the **influx** of newcomers taking over their land. Instead, the U.S. government sent troops to remove the Cherokee from the state.

On May 23, 1838, U.S. soldiers began to round up the Cherokee. The following month soldiers marched a small group of Cherokee west, eventually crossing the Mississippi River and reaching the Oklahoma Territory. By October the remaining Cherokee were marched out of Georgia in what became known as the "Trail of Tears," because of the suffering endured by the Cherokee.

THE CIVIL WAR

By 1860 about 460,000 African Americans lived as slaves in Georgia. Like other southern states, Georgia did not want to end slavery because slaves provided free or cheap labor. However, an increasing number of northern states opposed slavery. The nation became divided between pro-slavery and anti-slavery states. By 1860 it became clear that the conflict could not be settled by talk alone. On December 20, 1860, Georgia's neighboring state South Carolina became the first state to **secede** from the United States. Georgia quickly followed on January 19, 1861, joining the new **Confederate** States of America, which supported slavery.

The U.S **Civil War** began on April 15, 1861, when Southern soldiers attacked Fort Sumter, a Union army base located in the harbor of Charleston, South Carolina. The Civil War ended with a Union victory in 1865.

Sherman's March through Georgia

In May 1864 Union general Ulysses S. Grant ordered General William T. Sherman to attack inside "the enemy's country as far as you can." Sherman and his army fought south from Tennessee. They reached Atlanta in late summer and set it ablaze. The fire destroyed the South's railroad center and one of its largest cities. Leaving Atlanta in flames, Sherman and his troops cut a path of destruction across central and eastern Georgia to the Atlantic Ocean. After destroying farms and towns, Sherman arrived at Savannah on December 10th. A month later he left Georgia, heading north into South Carolina. He continued his march toward the Confederate capital at Richmond, Virginia, until the South surrendered in April 1865, ending the Civil War.

The 1863 Battle of Chickamauga was the worst Civil War battle fought in Georgia. The battle occurred in the northern mountains and lasted for two days. It was won by Southern troops. About 34,000 soldiers from the North and South died.

GEORGIA AFTER THE CIVIL WAR

Like the rest of the South, Georgia had to rebuild itself after the Civil War. This time in U.S. history is called the Reconstruction Era, because the country had to be reconstructed or put back together. The end of the Civil War brought an end to slavery. For the first time, African American men were allowed to vote and hold elected office. In the 1880s white-controlled state governments across the South passed **Jim Crow laws**. Some of these laws made it nearly impossible for African Americans to vote, so African American officeholders lost their positions. Other laws prevented African Americans from sharing schools, restaurants, hotels, or trains with whites. It took nearly 80 years for the Jim Crow laws to be overturned.

FAMOUS PEOPLE FROM GEORGIA

Margaret Mitchell (1900–1949), author. Born in Atlanta, Margaret Mitchell won the 1936 **Pulitzer Prize** for her only novel *Gone with the Wind*. The Civil War romance became one of the best-selling books of all time. Mitchell was hit by an automobile and died from her injuries.

Gone with the Wind *is the only novel Mitchell ever published.*

Jackie Robinson (1919–1972), baseball player. Jackie Robinson became the first African American to play major league baseball. He was born in Cairo. In 1947 he joined the Brooklyn Dodgers as its second baseman, helping the team win six National League titles in his ten seasons. Jackie's talent and courage became a model to many Americans.

Martin Luther King Jr. (1929–1968), civil rights leader. Martin Luther King Jr. was born in Atlanta, where both his grandfather and father were well-known **pastors** at Ebenezer Baptist Church. In 1954 he became the pastor at the Dexter Avenue Baptist Church in Montgomery, Alabama. In the late 1950s he became a leader in the **civil rights movement** and one of the most important African Americans in history. King was killed by an assassin in Memphis, Tennessee, in March 1968.

Ray Charles (1930–   ), singer. Born in Albany, Ray Charles lost his eyesight at age six because of an illness called glaucoma. He later studied music in Florida at the St. Augustine School for the Deaf and the Blind. Besides making the song *Georgia on My Mind* world famous, his other hits include *What'd I Say* and *Hit the Road, Jack.*

Jim Brown (1936–   ), football player. Jim Brown was born on St. Simons Island, off Georgia's coast. He was a star running back at Syracuse University in New York. He joined the Cleveland Browns in 1957, and he retired in 1966. He is third on the National Football League's (NFL) all-time rushing list.

Clarence Thomas (1948–   ), U.S. Supreme Court justice. Born in Savannah, Clarence Thomas became the second African American to serve on the U.S. Supreme Court. He grew up in a poor family and did well in school and college. He graduated from Yale University Law School in 1974. He won Senate approval to serve on the U.S. Supreme Court in 1991.

In 1949 Jackie Robinson was chosen as the Most Valuable Player in the National League.

A powerful speaker who believed in justice and nonviolence, Martin Luther King Jr. was awarded the **Nobel Peace Prize** *in 1964.*

Atlanta, Symbol of the New South

The **Civil War** destroyed most of Atlanta. After the Battle of Atlanta in 1864, only about 400 of almost 4,000 buildings remained standing.

REBIRTH AFTER THE CIVIL WAR

By 1870 the city was rebuilt. It had new buildings and businesses, including a new train station, which attracted newcomers to the reborn city. By 1870 Atlanta's population nearly tripled from what it had been in 1860. In 1860 about 7,500 people lived there, and in 1869 the population was more than 21,600. By 1890 the population nearly tripled again to 65,533. By the end of the

Few pre–Civil War buildings survived the burning of Atlanta. Consequently, brick buildings and early skyscrapers replaced wooden buildings.

1800s the city spread out to suburban communities, which were linked to the city center by streetcars powered by overhead electrical cables.

Part of the effort to rebuild Atlanta meant attracting new business. Newspapers such as the *Atlantic Constitution* promoted the city as the heart of the "New South" that was no longer governed by pre–Civil War viewpoints about class and race. By the mid-1880s Atlanta became the banking and railroad center for the southeastern states.

STRUGGLE FOR CIVIL RIGHTS

Martin Luther King Jr. grew up in an Atlanta neighborhood called Sweet Auburn. The Martin Luther King Jr. National Historic Site includes his birthplace, his church, and the Martin Luther King Jr. Center for Nonviolent Social Change, which was established in 1968 by King's widow Coretta Scott King.

Atlanta remains a place where African Americans play an important role in city life. It has the largest African American **middle-class** population of any large U.S. city.

Martin Luther King Jr. was a minister and a civil rights leader. The area of the Martin Luther King Jr. National Historic Site was the center of life for Atlanta's African American community in the early twentieth century.

Georgia's State Government

Georgia's state government is modeled after the U.S. government. It has three branches: the legislative, executive, and judicial.

LEGISLATIVE BRANCH

Georgia's **legislature** makes laws by voting on bills introduced by its members. It also is responsible for raising the money to pay for state services by passing tax bills. Taxes pay for public education, public roads, public health care centers, and maintenance of public parks and land.

The Georgia legislature is divided into two houses, or groups. The larger body, which has 180 members, is called the house of representatives. The smaller body, which has 56 members, is known as the senate. State representatives and senators serve two-year terms.

People in Dahlonega and Lumpkin County, site of the 1828 gold rush, collected 43 ounces of gold for the capitol dome. The gold traveled to Atlanta on a wagon train, where it was delivered on August 7, 1958.

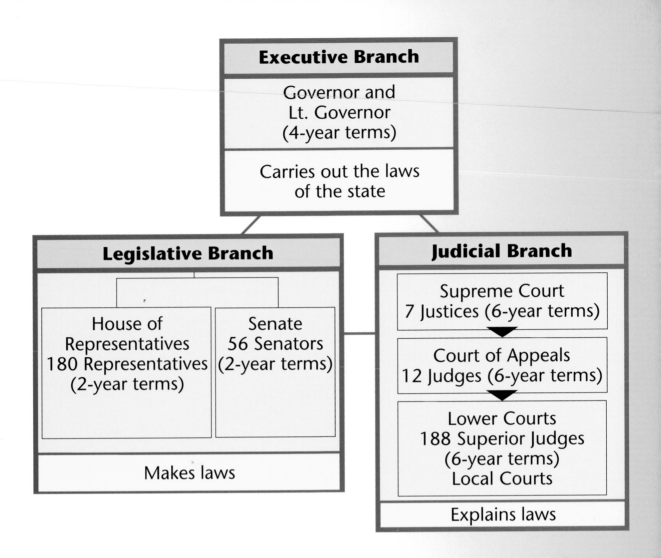

Executive Branch

Governor and
Lt. Governor
(4-year terms)

Carries out the laws
of the state

Legislative Branch

House of Representatives 180 Representatives (2-year terms)	Senate 56 Senators (2-year terms)

Makes laws

Judicial Branch

Supreme Court
7 Justices (6-year terms)

Court of Appeals
12 Judges (6-year terms)

Lower Courts
188 Superior Judges
(6-year terms)
Local Courts

Explains laws

EXECUTIVE BRANCH

The executive branch is led by the governor and enforces the state laws. The governor is elected by a statewide vote to a term of four years. The governor can only serve two terms. Along with the governor, other state leaders are elected to four-year terms. They include the lieutenant governor. He or she acts as state leader when the governor is away. The attorney general is the state's chief legal officer, and the secretary of state keeps the state records regarding births, deaths, and business licenses.

One Georgia governor, Jimmy Carter, was elected U.S. president in 1976. Carter came from the small town of Plains, served as a naval officer in the 1950s, and owned a peanut farm before running for office. He is the only Georgian ever elected president.

Georgia's Three Governors, 1947

For a few confusing weeks in 1947, three men each claimed to be Georgia's governor. The confusion began when the winner of the November 1946 election, Eugene Talmadge, died a month later, before taking office. His son Herman claimed his father's spot, based on support in the state legislature. The lieutenant governor, M. E. Thompson, disagreed. Thompson believed that because he still was second in command on Election Day, he should become the new governor. A third man, Ellis Arnall, had been governor until defeated by Eugene Talmadge. He claimed he should remain governor until the state supreme court ruled on the whole mess. Finally, the supreme court declared Thompson the governor because a majority of justices supported him politically. A year later, Herman Talmadge got his revenge when he defeated Thompson in a special election.

JUDICIAL BRANCH

The judicial branch interprets the laws that are passed by the legislature and enforced by the executive branch. The business of this branch takes place in the courts. Many cases, including those involving a crime or business disagreement, start at the local or superior court. These courts are found in every state county. Local voters elect superior court judges to four-year terms.

The court of appeals reviews decisions made by superior courts. The court of appeals may overturn, or change, the superior court decision if the lower court did not properly do its work in running the trial or interpreting the law. Court of appeals judges are elected and serve for six years.

The highest court is called the supreme court. It is the final interpreter of state law, hearing cases when people are not satisfied with the decision of the court of appeals. It also hears cases involving treaties or the Georgia or U.S. Constitution. Supreme court justices are elected and serve for six years. The justices elect the chief justice as their leader.

Georgia's Culture

The mix of Georgia's people, location, and history makes its culture unique.

WESTVILLE, TOWN FROM THE PAST

Westville, a **living history** village, shows how people in western Georgia lived 150 years ago. The people there dress in clothes and do jobs typical of the pre–**Civil War** South. Blacksmiths make horseshoes out of hot metal. Craftspeople weave baskets out of reeds. Woodworkers use hand tools to make furniture. Farmers use horses and plows to work the fields.

More than 30 buildings have been built in Westville to resemble how homes, schools, churches, and shops looked back in the 1850s.

GEORGIA STATE FAIR

A range of Georgia culture comes together at the state fair in Macon every September. The fair has been there every year since 1851, with the exception of four years during the Civil War. The fair brings together farmers and craftspeople from around the state.

Until the early 1950s no roads connected the coastal islands where the Gullah people lived to mainland Georgia. This allowed the Gullah culture to develop free from outside influences.

GULLAH CULTURE AND LANGUAGE

A unique culture can be found on a string of islands off the Georgia coast. The Gullah people are the descendents of **slaves**. The name Gullah probably came from Angola, one of the African countries from which slaves came. Over time, they developed their own language, a mix of old English and African speech. In Gullah, "Come with me" becomes "Come jine we." "Catch of the day" becomes "ketch ob de day." However, Gullah is more than simply a language. It is also a tradition of storytelling called "shout." The Gullah shout is a combination of drumlike rhythms and slave spirituals, or holy songs. To celebrate their culture, the Gullah people hold a festival every May.

Georgia's Food

Georgia's food is based on locally grown crops and livestock. Recipes come from African American, English, Native American, and other traditions.

SMOKEHOUSE HAM

Ham, or cooked pork, is a Georgia favorite. Smokehouse ham is pork that is slowly cooked, or smoked, with special spices to give it a tangy taste. In Georgia "slow cooking" means slow. Some smokehouse hams are cooked, or aged, for up to two years.

GEORGIA PEACHES

A dessert favorite is Georgia spiced peaches, which is a mixture of peaches, vinegar, cloves, and cinnamon. Together, they create a tangy flavor. Peaches are used for other desserts as well, including in pies and in homemade ice cream.

PEANUTS

Peanuts come from the same plant family as peas and beans. These plants have seeds that grow inside of pods. This vegetable family, called legumes, is a good source of protein, which is essential to good health. Georgia produces more peanuts than any

On April 7, 1995, the governor of Georgia signed an act declaring the peach as the state's official fruit.

other state—almost 40 percent of the nation's peanuts. Peanuts are a favorite for lunches or snacks. Other food uses for peanuts include making nondairy milk, cheese, ice cream, and especially desserts, including Georgia Peanut Butter Pie.

Georgia Peanut Butter Pie

Be sure to have an adult help you.

1 unbaked nine-inch pie shell

1 cup sugar

1/2 cup milk

1/2 cup peanut butter

1 teaspoon vanilla

2 eggs, separated

1 cup sweetened whipped cream

1/4 cup chopped peanuts

Preheat oven to 375°F.

Combine sugar, milk, peanut butter, vanilla, and egg yolks in a large mixer bowl. Beat on low speed until blended. In a small bowl whip egg whites until stiff. Fold stiffened egg whites into the peanut butter mixture. Transfer the mixture into the pie crust. Bake at 375°F for 30 to 35 minutes. Let cool to room temperature. Cover with whipped cream and sprinkle with chopped peanuts. Chill in refrigerator until served.

Georgia's Folklore and Legends

Georgia's folklore and legends reflect its rural traditions and its African American and Native American cultures. These tales are often not totally true but are based on bits of truth. They began as stories told around the fire or at gatherings. Over time they spread and became part of the community.

CROWS ARE IN THE CORN

One fine morning in Georgia, a farm family decided not to do their chores and sleep late. The crows did not mind. Usually the farmer was awake to scare them away from the corn growing in the field. Not this morning. The crows dropped into the field to enjoy some corn.

The farm rooster tried his best to wake the sleeping family. But the family slept on. The rooster screamed "Cock-a-doodle-doo! The crows are in the corn!" Still, the family slept on. Before long, the crows had eaten all of the corn, which is why in Georgia when people say, "The crows are in the corn," you better roll out of bed! This tale suggests that you better watch out for what belongs to you or else you risk losing it.

KEEPING THE BOO-HAG AWAY

For many years the Gullah people living on the coastal islands of Georgia had to battle a mean and ugly boo-hag, a type of monster. Like other boo-hags, this one was evil and worked for the devil. At night the boo-hag liked

to sneak into people's houses and do all sorts of things. The boo-hag would steal people's voices or cause them to have terrible nightmares. One of the boo-hag's tricks was to ride a sleeping person like a horse for miles. When the person finally woke up, he was more tired than before he went to sleep.

Finally a girl found a way to defeat the boo-hag that was bothering her family. One night before she went to bed, she left a broom on the floor. When the boo-hag came to her house, the boo-hag stopped to count every straw in the broom. Before the boo-hag knew it, it was sunrise. The boo-hag hated the light and fled, never to bother the girl or her family again. The girl learned to use her head, even when she was afraid.

THE DANCING BOYS AND THE SEVEN STARS

The Cherokee tell of seven boys who spent all of their waking hours dancing. Their parents told them to stop and do their chores, but the boys did not listen. Their parents decided to do something to stop the boys from dancing, and they approached the boys. To their astonishment, the parents saw most of the boys dancing in a circle while one boy beat on a drum.

The boys moved faster and faster as the drummer sped up the beat. Finally the boys and the drummer began to rise into the air. They climbed and climbed into the sky until they all became seven distant points of light forming a constellation. Today, some people say that the smallest star is the drum, but others think this star is the smallest of dancing boys.

Georgia's Sports Teams

Amateur sports, including college teams, have a long history in Georgia. As Atlanta's population increased in the mid-1900s, the city became able to support professional teams.

PROFESSIONAL SPORTS

The Atlanta Braves began play in 1876, and it is one of the oldest teams in baseball history. Until 1953 the team played in Boston, Massachusetts. In 1953 the team moved to Milwaukee, Wisconsin. They won the World Series as the Milwaukee Braves in 1957.

After moving to Atlanta in 1966, the Braves continued their winning ways. Sportswriters called it the Team of the '90s, because the Braves amassed twelve straight division titles between 1991 and 2003. The team also captured the National League title five times and won at least 100 games in five different years. It also won the 1995 World Series against the Cleveland Indians. The world championship title was the first for Georgia in any major professional sport.

The Braves play their home games at Turner Field, which is named after the team's former owner Ted Turner, who created CNN.

Masters Golf Tournament

Each year during the first week of April, one of the world's most famous golf tournaments takes place at the Augusta National Golf Club. The Masters began in 1934 when local golf legend Bobby Jones teamed with the Augusta Country Club to start the annual event. In 1935 Gene Sarazen hit "the shot heard 'round the world" scoring a **double eagle** on the par 5 15th hole. From 1965 to 1986 Jack Nicklaus won the Masters six times. The winner receives a green sports jacket, along with a trophy and large cash prize. In 1997 Tiger Woods broke the tournament four-day scoring record that had stood for 32 years.

The Atlanta Hawks of the National Basketball Association (NBA) did not begin in Atlanta. They started in 1946 as the Tri-Cities Blackhawks. The tri-cities are three neighboring cities on the Mississippi River—Moline and Rock Island, Illinois, and Davenport, Iowa. From 1951 to 1955 the team played in Milwaukee, Wisconsin. In 1958 it moved to St. Louis, Missouri, and renamed itself the Hawks. The Hawks moved to Atlanta in 1968. In 1982 the team acquired forward Dominique Wilkins, who had played at the University of Georgia. For a decade Wilkins was one of the best players in the NBA, earning the nickname the "Human Highlight Film."

Born in 1980, Michael Vick attended Virginia Tech before being drafted by the Atlanta Falcons in 2001.

One professional team that began in Atlanta is the NFL's Atlanta Falcons. The Falcons "hatched" on June 30, 1965. It took 25 years for the Falcons to become a championship team. In 1999 the Falcons won the National Football Conference title. They went on to play the Denver Broncos in the Super Bowl, and lost. Quarterback John Elway and former University of Georgia running back Terrell Davis led the Broncos to victory. A year later, the Falcons drafted college quarterback Michael Vick, who has emerged as one of the NFL's young superstars.

Anne Nguyen was a top player for the University of Georgia women's tennis team.

COLLEGE SPORTS

The South has a long tradition of college sports, especially football. The University of Georgia has had a football team since 1892. They have been national champions five times—in 1927, 1942, 1946, 1968, and 1980.

The football team is just one of the winning teams at the University of Georgia. The men's golf team were national champions in 1999, and the women's golf team won the title in 2001. The Bulldogs have won five national titles in gymnastics since 1987. The women's swimming and diving team won three titles in a row from 1999 to 2001. The men's tennis team won national titles in 1999 and 2001. The women's tennis team won the national championship in 1994 and 2000.

Georgia's Businesses and Products

INDUSTRY

In 1999 Georgia was fourth in the nation in the production of lumber. This lumber is used in building supplies and to make paper. The same trees are also used to produce half of the world's supply of important chemicals such as **resin** and turpentine, which are used in paint and other industrial products. The largest lumber company is Georgia-Pacific. Headquartered in Atlanta, it employs more than 60,000 people around the world.

Atlanta is also the home headquarters of other large corporations, including CNN, Delta Airlines, the United Parcel Service (UPS), and Coca-Cola.

Coca-Cola was invented in 1886 by Atlanta drugstore owner John Pemberton. He was trying to make a new cold medicine. Instead, he created Coca-Cola. The drink

The Coca-Cola Museum in Atlanta displays advertisements for the beverage that are more than 100 years old.

Vidalia onions have a higher sugar and water content than other onions.

became the basis for a corporation that now sells 70 different beverages in more than 200 countries. It has its own museum in downtown Atlanta, where visitors can learn about the history of the com-pany and sample many of the drinks it sells.

AGRICULTURE

Georgia leads the nation in the production of two popular nuts: peanuts and pecans. The pecan harvest is worth more than $103 million. Vidalia onions are the second most valuable state crop, bringing more than $84 million

Robert "Ted" Turner

Robert "Ted" Turner was born in Cincinnati, Ohio, in 1938. He moved to Georgia in 1963. For seven years he ran a company that put up billboards. In 1970 he bought TBS, a small television station in Atlanta. Ten years later he launched CNN, the first global TV news channel. CNN is one of the largest news organizations in the world, with more than 4,000 employees.

each year. Tomatoes are the third most valuable crop, followed by melons, bell peppers, cucumbers, sweet corn, and snap beans. More than 2.5 million peach trees on about 20,000 acres produce about 160 million pounds of fruit each year. The annual peach harvest is valued at $32 million.

Poultry, or birds raised as food products, contributes $12 billion each year to Georgia's economy. Georgia leads the nation in the production of broilers, or chickens raised to be eaten, and eggs. About two million broilers are produced yearly. Every week Georgia poultry farms ship more than 120 million eggs.

MINING AND QUARRYING

The 45 granite **quarries** in Elberton in northeastern Georgia make it the "Granite Capital of the World." Each year, they add $160 million to the state economy. No other place has so many granite quarries. Granite is a hard rock used for tombstones, memorials, kitchen countertops, and the outside of buildings. It comes in white, gray, brown, and other colors. The color depends on what other materials were fused with the granite when it was formed. Georgia white marble was used to make the statue of Abraham Lincoln in the Lincoln Memorial in Washington, D.C.

Georgia clay is dug or cut from the ground and is used to make pottery, paper, paint, rubber, plastic, and cat litter. Most of the clay is found in the Fall Line Hills. Georgia clay is even shipped to England, where it is used in the famous Wedgwood pottery.

Iron left in the dirt from eroding rocks is what makes the soil look red. People in central and northern Georgia use the clay to make pottery.

Attractions and Landmarks

While visiting Georgia, visitors can find many places of historical interest and natural beauty.

CIVIL WAR HERITAGE

Near Savannah is Fort Pulaski, a national monument. In April 1862 Union troops used a new type of cannon against the fort. This cannon had a longer range and was more accurate than those that came before it. It allowed the Union to take over the fort without sending many soldiers into it. Once the Union army took over, David Hunter, the general in charge, ordered the freedom of area slaves. Many of these African Americans joined the Union army to fight against their former masters.

The best preserved **Civil War** site in Georgia is the Altoona Pass Battle Site in the northern part of the state. It contains many mounds that were created when soldiers on both sides of the war built underground tunnels. At this site 2,000 Union soldiers guarded more than two million rations, or meals, for Sherman's approaching army.

Stone Mountain Park is best known for the sculpture of **Confederate** leaders Jefferson Davis, Robert E. Lee,

Stone Mountain Park contains the world's largest sculpture. The carving measures 90 feet by 190 feet.

Places to see in Georgia

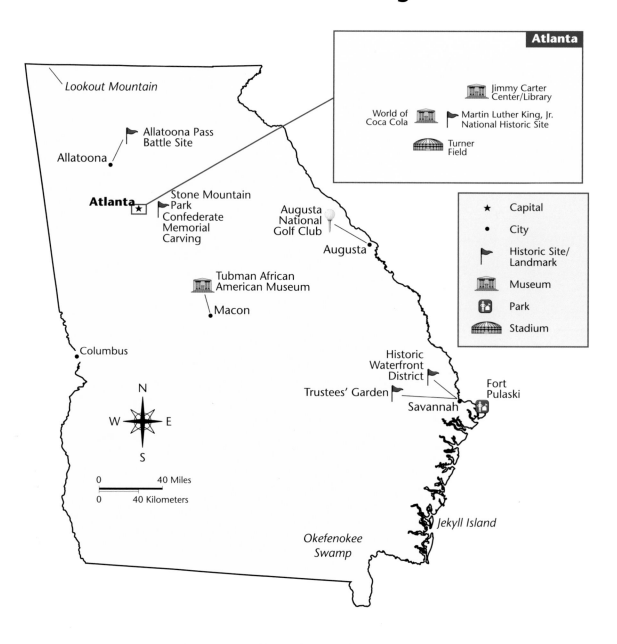

and Stonewall Jackson that is carved into its side. Some people call it the "Mount Rushmore of the South." The park, which also has miles of nature trails, attracts more than five million people each year. In 1924 President Calvin Coolidge signed a bill allowing the U.S. **mint** to make a special coin to help pay for the sculpting of Stone Mountain. The bill called for a specially designed half-dollar. Gutzon Borglum, who later created Mount Rushmore in South Dakota, was chosen to create the half-dollar's design. The head side shows the last meeting between Robert E. Lee and Stonewall Jackson. Shortly after their meeting in 1863, Jackson was accidentally shot and killed by his own men. The coin honored the men who fought for the Confederacy. More than two million coins were made, with all money going to turn Stone Mountain into the most famous outdoor art in the South.

HISTORIC SAVANNAH

Walking in Savannah's Historic Landmark District is like stepping back into the city's past. The district contains more than 1,100 homes and buildings that date back to the early 1800s. Within the district is the birthplace of Girl Scouts' founder Juliette Gordon Low. Many historians consider the Trustee's Garden the oldest U.S. garden, which dates back to the days of James Oglethorpe in the 1730s. The city also has a Historic Waterfront District lined with old cotton warehouses from the 1850s.

OKEFENOKEE SWAMP

The Okefenokee Swamp is the largest freshwater swamp in the United States. The name "Okefenokee" is a **Seminole** word that means "trembling earth." To protect the swamp, the government made it a refuge in 1937. The refuge covers about 396,000 acres, of which only 5 percent is dry land. The rest is a huge soggy **bog** crisscrossed by more than 120 miles of canoe trails. About 400,000 tourists visit the refuge each year.

The Okefenokee Swamp contains hundreds of different types of wildlife and is drained by the Suwanee and St. Mary's rivers.

The Tubman Museum has a collection of African artwork, including statues that date back 2,000 years.

JEKYLL ISLAND

One of the most popular spots along Georgia's southern coast is Jekyll Island. There visitors will find a tropical mix of palm trees, sand dunes, and live oak trees filled with hanging Spanish moss. Beginning in the late 1880s, the island was a retreat for some of the country's wealthiest families. Millionaires such as oilman John D. Rockefeller (1839–1937) and banker J.P. Morgan (1837–1913) built "cottages" that, in fact, are mansions.

AFRICAN AMERICAN HISTORY

Georgia's largest African American museum is the Tubman African American Museum in Macon. It was named in honor of Harriet Tubman, who is sometimes called the **Moses** of her people. A former slave herself, she led many slaves to freedom along the **Underground Railroad**.

The Carter Center, Atlanta

Jimmy Carter left the White House in 1981, after serving one four-year term as president. Nearly three years later, the Carter Center opened as part of a 35-acre park about two miles east of downtown Atlanta. The Carter Center is dedicated to promoting peace, human rights, and health care around the world. In 1987 the Jimmy Carter Library opened near the Carter Center. The library houses the papers and records, such as meeting notes and speeches, of Carter's years as president. Since leaving government, Jimmy Carter has remained active in the struggle for peace and justice. In 2002 he was awarded the **Nobel Peace Prize** for his many activities on behalf of human rights. He and Martin Luther King Jr. are the only winners from Georgia.

Map of Georgia

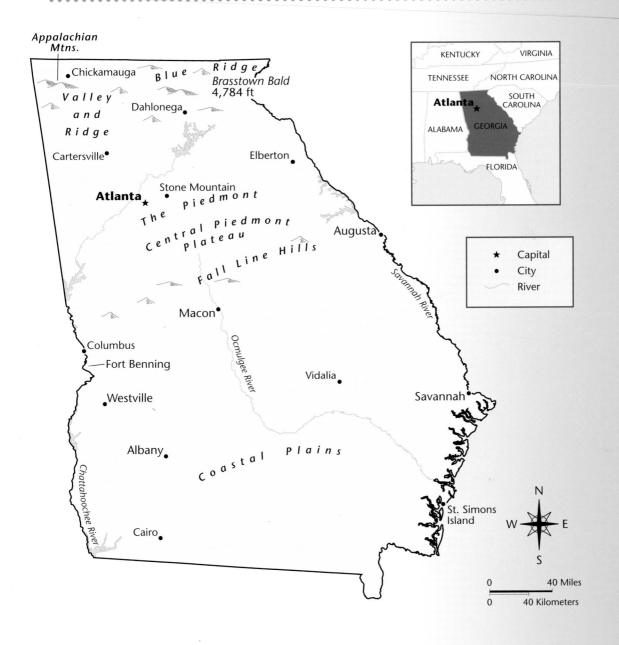

Appalachian Mtns.

Chickamauga

Blue Ridge
Brasstown Bald
4,784 ft

Valley and Ridge

Dahlonega

Cartersville

Elberton

Atlanta

Stone Mountain

The Piedmont

Central Piedmont Plateau

Fall Line Hills

Augusta

Savannah River

Macon

Ocmulgee River

Columbus

Fort Benning

Vidalia

Savannah

Westville

Albany

Coastal Plains

Chattahoochee River

Cairo

St. Simons Island

KENTUCKY   VIRGINIA
TENNESSEE   NORTH CAROLINA
Atlanta   SOUTH CAROLINA
ALABAMA   GEORGIA
FLORIDA

★ Capital
• City
⌇ River

N
W   E
S

0   40 Miles
0   40 Kilometers

Glossary

ancient   very old

bluff   a steep cliff

charter   a written document from a ruler or government, giving certain rights to a person or group of people

civil rights movement the fight for African Americans to gain voting and other rights during the 1950s and 1960s

Civil War   war within the United States between the Union (Northern, antislavery states) and Confederacy (Southern, proslavery states) from 1861 to 1865

Confederate   the Confederate States of America is what the Southern states that left the Union in 1861 called themselves

double eagle   when a golf player completes a hole three strokes less than par. For example, a good golfer is expected to complete a par five hole with five strokes; a golfer scoring a double eagle completes it with two strokes.

drone   male bee that has no stinger. Its function is to mate with the queen bee.

endangered   at risk of being gone forever, such as a plant or animal with a sharply declining population

exports   goods or products sent to another country

infantry   the branch of an army made up of people trained to fight on foot

influx   a flowing in

Jim Crow laws   laws passed by southern legislatures to prevent African Americans from voting

legislature   government officials elected from local parts of a state to write and pass laws and control state funds

living history   people dressing and acting in ways of the past

middle class   the people who make an amount of money that puts them above the working class but under the wealthy

mint   a government building used to make coins

Moses   biblical character credited with freeing Jewish slaves in Egypt and leading them back to their homeland in present-day Israel

Nobel Peace Prize   annual award given by the Swedish government to recognize achievement in fields such as peace, literature, chemistry, biology, economics, and medicine

pastor   a minister or priest

Protestant   a member of a non-Catholic Christian church

Pulitzer Prize   annual award given to recognize achievement in literature and journalism

quarries   open spaces from which stone is obtained by digging, cutting, and blasting

rapids   fast-moving river water

resin a liquid that comes from a plant that is used in paint, ink, and plastics

Seminole Native American tribe living in present-day northern Florida and southern Georgia

slaves people who are owned by and forced to work for someone else

slavery the condition of being a slave

threatened species a plant or animal that is not in danger of disappearing altogether but may be in danger in the near future if not protected from harm

transplanted moved from one place to another

Underground Railroad secret paths that slaves took north to freedom

wetland low area heavy in water, such as a swamp or marsh

worker bee female bee that helps the queen bee

More Books to Read

Jacobs, Jimmy. *Moonlight through the Pines: Tales from Georgia Evenings.* Marietta, Ga.: Franklin-Sarrett Publishers, 2002.

Lightle, Bill. *Made or Broken: Football and Survival in the Georgia Woods.* Bloomington, Ind.: 1st Books Library, 2002.

Lommel, Cookie. *James Oglethorpe: Humanitarian and Soldier (Colonial Leaders).* Broomall, Pa.: Chelsea House Publishers, 2000.

Smothers, Ethel Footman. *Down in the Piney Woods.* Grand Rapids, Mich.: Eerdmans Publishing, 2003.

Index

About the Author

Larry Bograd is the author of numerous books for children and young adults. He lives in Denver, Colorado, but has visited Georgia many times. He has seen the Atlanta Braves play at Turner Field, toured the Coca-Cola Museum and Underground Atlanta, and bought a quilt in the northern mountains.

GIVEN BY
FRIENDS OF
CHEROKEE COUNTY
PUBLIC LIBRARIES